*To Brenda
with much thanks and
admiration. —*

The Day of the Three Swans

Edward Boyne

Edward Boyne.

Doire Press

First published in September 2010.

Doire Press
Aille, Inverin
Co. Galway
www.doirepress.com

Editing: John Walsh
Cover design & layout: Lisa Frank
Cover photo: Jocelyn Murray Boyne
Author photo: Jocelyn Murray Boyne

Printed by Clódóirí Lurgan Teo.
Indreabhán, Co. na Gaillimhe

ISBN 978-1-907682-02-5

Dedicated to Janet and Jocelyn.

Acknowledgements

Acknowledgements are due to the following journals and newspapers in which versions of some of these poems first appeared:*Cyphers, Poetry Review, Crannóg, Ropes, The Sunday Tribune, The SHOp* and *The Cúirt Journal.*

Special thanks to the members of The Writers' Keep, Galway.

Contents

Herengracht

Permanent waters lick the city's sinews
out of a stubborn obligation,
pausing to admit the sheddings of the streets.
We're not afraid of the deep lost colours,
the flat brown of old conversations.

There are no imaginable fish.
Nothing could penetrate
that confident obsolete liquid
sucking reliably under every bridge.
Perhaps distant thunder — but that too is missing.

Stories float downwards like sediment
to compensate for the absent mountains,
and our scheduled squandered evenings,
irrigated by Merlot and random giddiness,
are not defects in the prevailing arrangements.

Freud

The first couch, a patience zone.
Familiars interrogated, slide into trance.
Shadows are claimed as vices.

Memory is heated under pressure,
gathers too fast
in menacing side-pools.

The only known maps show
impassable false trails.
You have to be foolish

or heart-worn, and hope,
with little to sustain your hope,
this place is possible.

You torture accidental words,
the blank wall for company,
his bearded breath at your shoulder,

and the first rules hold:
legs open before language; desire
hums through the frayed cables of the anxious.

The Art of Love

The art of love is the same
as the art of war.
Attack where there is no defence,
defend where there is no attack.

Don't rush to specifics.
Be wary of satellite photographs.
Double reconnaissance,
track subtle frequencies,
wait until the contours
of her perimeter
shape the daylight,
and then wait more.

Beware of her decoys
and under-lit diversions,
false surrenders, mobile armour,
the deadly accuracy
of remote intention,
the invisible massing of scorn
on her borders.

But don't wait too long.

Go in hard when you go.
Advance in a single gesture
at the least sign of distraction.
Deploy overwhelming mystery.
Take only unnecessary prisoners.

Palamari

('Abandoned BC 1750 after 800 years
continuous habitation. Reason unknown.')

1

The sun is your last fortification
at this blazing afternoon hour.

Revealing the streets, more maze
and hive-like than I'd guessed.

None can now invoke your enemies
but reckon they were relentless,

from the joined fists of your walls,
your back-to-the-ocean stance,

worked flints and pared arrowheads
scattered, sharpening all approaches.

2

A girl in a white tunic on the worn pier
wears an ankle-bracelet of beaten silver,

rests her fly-worried water-urn
on the flat of an upturned boat.

The afternoon sleeps, silent as history.
Nearby new, anchored, nodding warships.

Bangkok

How night is an electric panic of cars.

How tight horizons are burned by headlights.
How streets are resented furrows cut.

How street-stalls interrupt,
assemble blockages, eye the latest catch,
caught in the snare of display.

How the crushing flux
for the moment's fix
suffocates.

How the children walk to school on boiling streets,
the home spirits not all left.

How only those with pure heart will survive
and those without will prosper.

How wounds dry inwards in the motor dust.

How a city of speedometers, thermometers
takes the measure of moisture and moving air.

How cars are an element like wind and sun,
how blood is the colour of risk,
how water isn't plentiful and retreats at daybreak.

Beach

The miles of loosened grit
between rock and sea, cupped suburb
and water storm. Gulls binge at dawn
among apple cores and cola cans.
The beach could love them like a blanket
if it were spring. It leans
into the dainty webs of their feet.

Damp sand grieves for beach-towels,
bottles buried neck-deep ponder waves.
The sand suckles flies,
seaweed frisked by gales.
The sea is its brisk conversation,
sea-sound, vowels rolled, holds long,
echoing finally like pain.

Its dream is still fresh-water,
a feed of soils, seed digging in, seed
the way it used to be,
forcing itself naked into ground.

Late evening, summer, the full head thins
to scattered human flesh-sticks against sky blue,
threads of dark in a passing cloud,
near bollocksed dunes a tree from Beckett.
The tramps are sun-burnt pink, expansive,
and lie with shorts and opened flies.

Beyond sand hills, towns brace to reclaim
kids dozing in cars, their heads damp,
tastes of the tongued and the seen,
full as buckets with the day.

Darkness brings the lovers,
multiples of fingers grip breasts, cocks,
dunes slide and groan like bullocks,
sand roughens in flesh, cars sink,
shaking windless nights on springs,
discarded rubbers puddle wet,
lit carefully by refracting dawn,
the dawn's colours reflected and honed,
when beach sand and morning meet.

Blitz

Remember the minnows we tortured,
billy-can over a fire of tiny branches.
They darted faster as the heat burst
the gradual water bubbles and we laughed.

I saw children's bodies in rows
like oatmeal sacks, the rats enquiring.
Blown buildings, scattered bricks,
a long tantrum from the brutal air.

Saw a headless girl hunkering
by a low whitewashed wall,
her clothes burned off,
a sprawl of bloodied piss at her feet.

We got used to living underground,
the long slippery tiled steps down
into a silence broken by wails
from hungry babies, the random drip of water.

Remember how we talked all night
around a larger fire. The dry air,
the canopy of stars giving us courage
to see and almost touch with words.

I swamped the broken bodies,
the sky noise, the bloodied rubble
in the blue of work and drink, craved
the ceaseless flooding of the nerves.

Excavation
(At The Neale, Mayo, 2006)

No ordinary dyings these, spinal cords hacked
clean at the neck while likely still alive,
jagged vertebrae, missing index fingers.
They lived in their skins, their only earthly home.
Evening travellers surprised by wary guards,
or castle prisoners chopped late after due torture.

The young students stroke thigh bones lovingly
with long-bristle brushes, sharpened scrapers,
mysterious annotations, academic incantations.
Note the bones in Christian position facing eternity,
soil and the damp ecumenism of discovery.
The once-anointed skulls, their lost expressions
never held by mirrors, housed readers of dusk,
of stilled vibrations, the sharper resonances of night.

Old flinty pelvises put brakes on a road widening,
on the sacred increments of acceleration,
the hallowed private momentums.
A month's delay for each strayed century.
They are reborn from clay to a fresh resentment.

Café

I'm surrounded by sugar-bowls, chipped,
empty salt-shakers. The sauce bottles
have beards from neglect and promiscuity.
So many hands, different knives,
the workings of diverse tongues and tastes.

All the lovers I'll never regret are here.
They have long elegant hair and give me looks,
gently suggestive of the after-life.
Others too, the smilers, the frowners.
The pathways filled to bursting.

My patient stares chase each slow second
across their eyes, onto the tremor of their grip,
the silver of suspicious sweat between nostril and lip.
In their careful inattention, they don't allow
for being so securely interrogated.

My father, his father and all possible fathers.
My mother, her mother and all impossible mothers.
I never ask that they account for their animation.
They don't know how a mind emptied out
has space to suck them in completely.

How lately I only need six types of armour,
depending on the blood-group,
as protection from them. I have a mind-switch too,
fast as a yawn, that can blank them out.
I can tell how dry their throats get.

Encounter

A deep-throat wail in the flat night
sounds like an angry human child
adrift in the taut city.
I shine my torch
onto the balcony of 24b,
meet jungle-tipped eyes,
ancient feline wariness.

The pause
is the length
of many passing cars.

I'm quickly out-of-bed-cold
but neither of us wants to make
that first revealing move.

Cat eyes return the electricity,
combine trigger-readiness
with the deepest knowing,
indifference.

I'm forced to feel appraised
and disrespected
in a bare-foot stand-off
by a conceited creature
with no postal address
or registration plate.

Celery

Ten men, ten beds, tight air.
The tired intimacy of bedpans
old pyjamas, illicit fag-smoke, piss.
Tony, his leg bolted in three places,
Arthur in an aluminium neck brace,
Noel with both legs raised by pulleys.
A long-haul crew, wedded
to the merciful mysteries of screws,
metal plates, reluctant bones.

I hadn't imagined it would be here,
a place of grudging healing.
There was no other bed after they found
those untameable cells touring your spine.

Each day as I turned in the door
your washed-to-grey socks accused me.
Those cheap acrylic socks, a present
when I was twelve, on your useless feet.

Your hairless shins lay like protesting celery
over the white hospital quilt.
Property of Beaumont Hospital
embroidered on it in red.

The hospital hairdresser charged too much.
John Major was the worst wanker yet.
Criminals were taking over in the newspapers.
Lunch was another ward's leftovers.

2

Sister Callinan drew portable curtains
loose around your bed. She lit a candle
near your face. I sat on a ward chair
by the shy flame as the day thinned.

Your beyond-familiar face was closed
as seasoned wood.

'Let me go,' you said at the last,
and went.
A measure of our bond
that I could hold you back?
Or you had a chance to stay
a little longer and declined?
I'll never know,
but ahead of yourself as always,
getting it over with early.

Suddenly you were past going.
The moment burned with itself,
there was no breath for breathing.

The most recent ward recruit,
a centre forward with a busted knee,
invisible to me in the next bed,
boasted to silent visitors:
'I saw it coming all day. I knew.'

Cemetery Facts

Poets in tomb-granite have blithely dispensed
with the seven rules for the use of capitals.

Scant space to linger between grave-borders,
consolations are exposed to cold erosions:

Unlived youth vanished like Sketches on sand,
Spared Middle-Age; Eternally We cherish.

Portrait photos embossed on grave-granite,
the now too mortal face, lit in a camera flash,
sharing a bad joke, grinning, pretend-enthusiastic,
not taking offence or asserting cranky rights.

I run my finger along one joint between plastic
and stone where an optimistic snapshot found a home.

One fuzzy moment shoved the someone into frame,
radiant and worm-food in the blowing rain.

Consumption

(Henrietta St, Dublin, 1931)

My lungs are cracked glass and the cold air
cleaves through me like sunlight.

No doctor, but Sadie from the corner
who worked as a cleaner in the Adelaide
and knows the cough by its raspy sound
and the way the skin goes like dried white cabbage.

My sister Philo brings me soup in the bed,
boiled potato peels and broccoli stalks.
She always has a story from the market stall
and a hankie to her nose and mouth.
She fusses around my bed like guilt on legs.
When she's gone her scent hangs in the room
along with the dust no cleaning ever clears.

I've lain here for over a year, dreading the winter,
when my little window-panes get frost-stained
and fill with terrible dark by afternoon.

I dreamed this room was once a pantry
where the butler with a rose in his lapel
groped the frilly parlour-maid.
Her notorious pale breasts were fed
on fresh pheasants, venison from the Phoenix Park,
apple dumplings, stray bananas, the leavings of trays
and flower-decked banquet-tables.
If I don't breathe I can hear
the faded revving of their throaty laughs.

I get up in the night for the pot, legs like stale bread,
brittle to the touch and white, thin as well.
'Fifteen-year-old God bait,' my Philo says
when she has a few jars on board.
That gets me laughing,
and I need to laugh.

Endgames

Back then you were reaching
for certainties and dry consolations.
There was too much pressure
in a look, too much old hold
in a sudden edgy hug.
Skin charged out of habit,
then diffused, unused,
no longer finding vehemence
in the rare force of the other.
Passion had been a fire composed
of numerous raw coals
now deliberately made scarce.

We agreed, I suppose we had to,
that survival was refusal,
cut and spliced the reel to endure,
left dark episodes in unmarked graves.

Lately, I've had to deduce
you've left a room by the afterglow,
the way air-currents reassemble
after circling a tense presence,
the ruffled furniture's exchange
of glances. It's become impossible
to find you by looking harder.

We arrived together that last time
at repeating episodes of self-scrutiny,
inventories were taken at one remove,
balance sheets of unnecessary damage,
our exchanges hardened into evidence,
grist for the chilly stage of parting.

The episodes joined together
to give us evenings of wary sadness
and stilted, unending days.
I can feel the same approach again.
I would spare you all of it
if I could spare myself.

Final Evidence

Nothing original,
particles of deceased skin
suspended in the cool air.

Nail clippings
alive in the overflow.

Rusted two-bar heaters,
pawed books from the same
demolished bed-sit.
That half-moon coffee stain,

shrubs arranged perfectly.
Children who want to be different,
over-worn clothes,
washed-to-grey underwear,
smooth stone shapes
found by the sea shore.

A new window in a wall,
a canoe like a wooden boil
on the spring grass. Indent
of buttocks in a favourite chair.

Ash from a pipe,
small change in a jacket,
over-read letters from him
or her. Contraband joys
settled like glass.
Abandoned passions.

Blood samples
in the distant laboratory,
where parting
is predicted,
not postponed.

Christmas Morning

The twelve-year-olds have new shiny suits,
box-creased Ben Sherman shirts, shaved heads,
ride mountain bikes between the clothes-lines.
Younger ones fire new battery guns;
plastic glows electric, strafing the playground
and a defenceless leaden sky.

Two burnt-out cars redden in the lower courtyard
near McCabe's flat and Our Lady's Grotto.
There are still black scorch-marks
on the concrete where they gushed flame
and angry smoke at Halloween.
Our Christmas turkey roasts in gas-fired silence.

Next door a loud row already
between a man and a woman, or maybe two men
and a woman. Mam says: 'Turn up
that telly and close the window to the balcony.'
I can hear their razor-voices,
a growl of rage at the sober-bright morning.

The circus is on, recorded in Russia.
Girls in tutus somersault on a single tight-rope,
their waists full with furry plumage, their arses tight,
too distant for credit or amazement.

Mam slips out, wearing her oven gloves,
to lift used needles from the balconies.

Film Noir

1

Consider this:
a back-street hotel,
smoky redbrick and a side-alley
with rusted, overflowing bins.
A desk-clerk from film noir
wears a stiff black moustache
and has seen it all before.

The sheets are usually clean
and the spotted mirror
over the dressing-table
has shown no better days.
The tinted front windows,
with views of a cultured wino
in the doorway across the street
singing arias and cursing Dante,
are cleaned twice a year.

Lovers come at midnight
without luggage or answers.
There's a font for lemon
and salt on each landing,
and a special knock the waiters
use for delivering house champagne
and plates of pleasingly thin,
lavishly-oiled French fries.

From the start there's been rumours
someday they'll knock it down,
sell off the old bricks for hardcore,
build a shopping mall
made from tall glass and sell
cardigans, cheap underwear.

2

They closed the hotel without warning.
There's a notice today
in *The Chronicle*, the column
beside 'Agricultural Implements'.
The guests found in flagrante
were given directions to the suburbs,
spare toothbrushes,
instructions on dental hygiene,
vouchers for solid fuel,
unofficial apologies.

There'll be an auction soon,
blankets, ceiling-mirrors, lamps,
in-house hairdryers,
black velvet sheets (used).

Expect souvenir hunters,
bearded nostalgists, the curious,
those who lacked courage
when it was forever open.

Voice Lessons at the Academy

What I remember
about that place:
three stories up
calf-biting stairs
grey stacking-chairs
arranged like hands
at the room's throat
white walls flayed
and etched with a thousand
dancers' kicks and landings.

Our voice lessons:
'In-breath to a count
of ten.'

The raw lungs ratcheted
forced open.

'Exhale with an aaah!'

Sounds blown
through secret tunnels
gathered outside us
like passions.

 'Can you go uuuu
to a count of twenty?'

Not in my driest moments.
But I hummed her lips
from a thousand miles
across the floor.

In-breath again
this time for twenty.
I felt my toes redden.
'Send your sound
to the far corner.'

I thundered
down the ten scales
of wanting
to a whistle
bred for music.

This parted her eyelids further.

We exhaled always to the screams
of thin brakes, lorries outside
the shivery windows
wet traffic, dark downpours,
lives in overcoats below.

My mind a clenched jaw
my air heavy as leather
never close enough to her breath.

Fire Water

The annals have it that on Ardee Street
a bonded warehouse caught fire one night.
It was 1875. My grandfather wasn't born.
His father saw the smoke from darkest Bride Street.

Bottles blew up in the heat. Barrels disgorged
streams of burning liquor down Ardee Street.
It was as if the Gates of Paradise had opened.
The Liberties awash in 20-year-old best malt.

People jammed the storm-drains with old coats,
mattresses from prams, logs from Donoghue's yard.
Carts, stranded, blocked all approaches to Ardee Street
in case helmeted help arrived too soon.

When the whiskey flowed fire-free, mouths opened
showing blackened teeth, tongues lapped,
bony bodies prostrate faced the flow.
The party swam all night around Ardee Street.

Scores of the happy-pickled had to be dragged up
from gutter-heaven by the day shift of the DMP,
cursing and swearing. 'For your own safety. For drunk
and disorderly. For breaching the Queen's peace.'

First Drink

It was more of an anointing.
The barman in 'The Ramble Inn'
was tipped off the night before.
I was to be fifteen, not legal,
but the right age to open an account
with the tribe's way of pre-meditated
forgetting, airless flight, simultaneous
inflation and decline. My father slyly
included me in the round and not:
'A mineral for the young lad in the lounge.'

I knocked it back faster than he liked.
My show-off way to say it's not my first,
just the first with you, and I can drink you
under any table you might name, Da.

Old artisans of oblivion stood near
enough to listen, supportive and apart,
hair growing from their nostrils and ears,
the authority of time served etched
on their faces, frowning in approval.

Hawk

The young hawk hovering
for hours over Skyros town
with the noon sun blasting,
had checked me out.

Dry-haired, furrow-faced,
sprawled over a loud deck-chair
on a white-washed roof,
looking the wryly persistent
offender in my pose,
distant weather rumbling
inside me.

Sorry to be awake.

She gauged my balding
crown, too reddened
for much wisdom. The rest
not worth locking onto.

What's always at stake
is the swooping
hawk
the unflown air.

Italian Train in March

The fog is local, hanging around the back slopes
while the ground gives up its winter damp.
Random cypresses punctuate the fields,
precarious brick-houses, medieval grain-stores,
sudden blocks of flats with washing
hanging down from windows, the roofs
connected by armoured cables brought down
the valleys on minor Eiffel towers.

Women are framed in tiny doorways, men
look definite in the distant cabs of tractors.
The waiting ground is not yet burnt.
The cattle are jet black and perfect.

We slow through yards, pass passive stations,
gutted car-shells redden in the shadows,
quicken into open hill-country, pear trees
grip the slopes in endless ordered rows.

I doze with the mute sameness of pears
and hear your voice from the remoteness
of the seat across, chanting softly to itself,
that portable, home-hugging, cautious song.

Notes from a Washington Suburb

I'm sitting unshaven on the front steps at five.
It's all men driving past at this hour.
Most drivers look me over, twice.
I must be doing something unusual.

The houses have come together to sleep
and not much else. I hear a hose
caress a lawn in the next street. Makes me
wonder about average rainfall, water meters.

Joggers fast tip-toe in shorts and bright Nikes,
pass each other without a word.
It was the same yesterday at this hour.
Now the night breeze is picking up.

The silence hereabouts is purposeful.
It's been the case a long time.
Could be the main events will all conclude
without us and without comment.

I'm watching a squirrel scale an electricity pole,
its brown pelt against the pale weathered wood.
A poster showing last month's latest 'Missing Child'
fades back to paper in the quickening air.

Photographs from the 1930's
(San Francisco Museum of Modern Art, 1994)

The worry-pinched face of a teenage girl
hugging three nippers with matted hair,
sleepy faces. Her brother and sisters?
They have woken up fully-clothed
in the black vinyl back of a model T.
Drought and drought-dust blowing
into the whites of their unshielded eyes
sent them hungry to that sun-washed coast.

I pause beside a tour guide
in a black leather skirt.
A knot of Japanese men follow her
in step on a company trip,
wearing tight grins, name tags, cameras.

She points to a larger, more faded print.
'This is famous…' Eight men and three boys
standing to attention on a dusty road,
their faces scrubbed-up to morning hope.
The bosses watching behind the camera
are about to choose for the day.

The Nikons point and the room is flash.

Rat

(Mountjoy Square, 1920)

A rat's wet mouth
clamped on my sleeping nipple
and sucked, rat-sucked
my child's milk.

In the cold space
that hung between
my warm dream
and his long tail,
I thought it was
your chapped lips
tight on my soft flesh.

Sleepy I reached a hand
for your curly head.
It paused,
tense in its fur.

The baby snuffled
in her cardboard cot,
licked lips with a milky tongue.

I gripped pulse,
wet fur,
my closed fist.

Refugee

I empty my bladder
near a shellhole,
where the gorse is burnt
to pubic black.
My haunches tense
against weeds, the prickly
eyes of men.

The sycamores
are blasted bare
as wires.
Tall and short ones
like a family.
The light is fierce
in the angle
of their branches.

I have carried a rope
and a bag of clothes
across borders since dawn.
The soles of my feet are raw.

The scents are truck fumes
and falling smoke.

They took turns with me
for two cold days.

The sun is high enough,
this road too full.

This branch will hold
for long enough.
The rope is warm
against my jaw,
it comforts my ears.
I have tied
my hair back.

Sniper Near Aughnacloy

Alone up here,
the electric burr of radio silence,
the damp patience of crushed grass,
the breeze sharp against my open eye,
the finger-intimacy of a rifle trigger.
The road below is a grey scar
through green scrub, bog; nervous
convoys falter at the bend.

These new sights cut bodies into quarters.

I don't know the timing of thunder
or the wavelength of tracer fire.
I know the heat of a lamb's breath,
the snail's spittle trajectory.

I know it entered his ear like a dark wind.
A thin boy, fresh from Leeds,
with a recruit's shaved head.

I finger squaddies' heads like worry beads.

Suspicion

I suspect the long sit of cattle chewing,
repeating the same dull whispers,

the conspiracies of leaves floating
on deadlocked flood-pools,

the whistling behind chimney-breasts,
giving false shape to the wind,

the nostalgia for burnt-out buildings,
the brown of parched grass threatening green

in early autumn downpours.

I suspect autumn,

all so-called natural decay,
cycles of birth and dying,

the tight knowing of crushed reeds,
the shadows that grow behind laughter.

I suspect laughter,

the too-tight handshake
with practised eye contact,

my name repeated back to me,
as advised in the sales manuals,

all talk of Internet and e-mails,

messages left without voices,
voices left without messages,

the new magic in megabytes.

I suspect megabytes,

the digital certainties on a bright screen,
the pre-meditated tear in an eye,

the women who drift without anchor
and the men who support them,

the men who pretend they are lost
and the women who find them.

I suspect all honing of the spirit,
incense, tabernacles, chanting,

processions of the worthy,
men in slow robes
who question my innocence.

Swallow

I had blundered into the long barn
in search of rope and a piece
of metal with a cutting edge,
when a sudden nesting swallow
amplified the force of my intrusion,
flew between rafters, cut corners,
at an outdoor speed,
threw herself into an unequal contest
with the massed angles of the interior,
repeated doomed circlings of the overhead
rough-cut rafters,
dipped in flight, broke her neck against
the smudged glass of a closed window.

The Great Pyramid of Mayo
(Built 1786 at The Neale)

He fashioned a crude sentence
in rough cut stone
out of the grammar of grief;
unloaded the mannered
Egyptian afterlife
onto the plains of Mayo,
its fixed churches
and reticent prospects,
its armoured understandings.

No knowing how far
the impulse spread,
the River Robe the Nile,
Claremorris was maybe Cairo,
Karnak was Castlebar.
The meanings at their widest
near high ground,
otherwise a perfect secret.

Crows took turns to visit
by day, at dusk the light
clatter of bats was heard
circling the impulsive apex.
The builders laughed up sleeves,
into their cups. Told brazen
women by night in Ballinrobe,
about fools and good money.

Lately the locals nibble
at his canvas edge,
for new bungalows, dog kennels,
children's swings, extensions.

With their seed-like eyes
and indoor tans,
watch the hallowed glow
from Hollywood after dark.
Stand accused of little.

The Day of the Three Swans

I dwelt in that other yellow place
for thirty wet years.
Locals called it 'The Mental'
though I wasn't from those parts,
nor were any of my people
who never found the gates.

There was a long wall, so tall
it was hard to tell what kind of day
had fallen in among us.
I'm certain the place
was warm in a foolish way.

I caught every smiling stranger
wandering the scrubbed halls
in black and white, like a negative
held up to the known light,
the way you can see what shapes
are there, and what they want,
and spot the shades
that colour takes away.

My favourite corridor
opened onto spring apples, flower bunches,
frostless lake-water, tyre tracks.
Pill-trolleys-fronting-nurses
prowled the wards for mouths.

I stayed quiet when I heard
their apple voices tempt
the gathered snakes.

When I took their pearly offerings,
my bones weighed less than thought.

The day's texture was stringy
as cabbage or a mother's bacon.
No two days were different
except the day of the three swans.

Near my long silences, my walls of safety,
lay the banging of pans, steel tray collisions,
glass bottles chattering in crates,
the sound of cleaners humming to themselves
like traffic growing nearer.

The nurses graced us in shifts,
eloped at tea-time in long coats,
collected by a green bus that never washed,
its metal jaws held open as it left,
even when winter blew shivers off the lake.

I saw them through diesel smoke,
stretched across the long bus window,
like a queue that never moved,
looking back at us, not longingly,
gradually remote and homeward turned.

I met everything before it came,
and had it gone before it went.

Shrine on the Road North

The road became a bridge over bog,
green layers, brown boils, light sweat,
oak and metals smothered under asphalt.

The bog sucked at our vision.
Our metal bubble of silenced air
revved from pole to pole,
tall out of yellow rushes, the peat
turned over near the road-verge
like a grave, burnt bellies
of sheep, silver farm gates' endless
privacies, farmhouses stiff
with allegiance, the mortar grey
where stone leant on stone, sills
cocked to split a southerly wind,
unpersuaded timbers,
until a town's indecisive edges,
roadside shrine,
a statue's arm, upraised, pointing
skywards, warning of cruel weather,
enclosed by railings, shiny
kneelers, new varnished pine,
shadows reducing daylight by a wall,
another pale plaster figure, head bent,
cowled, unarmed, praying in the rain.

Brush

In the shoeless pause after tea,
she swept the kitchen lino,
patrolled between us and the television,
butt-smoking, jerky interference,
no tuning knob could tackle.
We strained necks to watch 'The Fugitive',
behind, to the side, in her wake,
to second-guess the way of the brush,
keep telly in view and track
how Richard Kimble made
another escape.

Her eyes stayed down, locked
like suction on the patterned floor;
her insistent unilateral strokes
probed for alien invaders, dust clusters,
coils of fluff escaped from justice,
breadcrumbs strayed from the knife,
little gashes of sticky muck
from water-logged building sites.

Her dowager's hump gave her the look
of an aproned crow on a stick,
back-bone brittle as a pencil
tense between clenched fists.

My weathered father and me,
long-trousered, silent comrades,
had to prop our stockinged feet,
like four stuffed bears on the same small stool.

Missile

Much later a flunky in faded green overalls,
sweaty on overtime, wheeled my trolley
along disinfected corridors with locked doors
that led into life. He had a small face
and neatly manicured hands. Not a warrior.
One of the trolley's wheels was buckled,
wobbled from side to side, making me vibrate.

The drawer, my new home, winked shut.
Closed and stored, the strain of gravity lifted,
I could sense the liquid settle in my vertebrae.
My skin was grey as unloved semolina.

Nothing happened before this, I did not travel
or find anyone. There were no loves or hatreds.
No passions or great failures. I didn't risk my body
in the fight. That steely drawer and later
a satin-lined wooden crate, shaped like a missile.

Moorehall

(Destroyed by Irregulars during The Irish Civil War, 1923)

The ruined hulk speaks through jackdaws,
the scent of friends, half-intact bays,
memories of raw servants baking bread,
scrubbing, dreading the sweat-primed dawns.

Burnt because it wasn't a thatched hut.

The brambles are bad-tempered at the rain's
stance. Glassless windows disappoint the light,
edges cut the air, defiant and tight with stone,
where brittle plaster felt the strain and fell.

Burnt by the small men with revolvers.

Massed fir trees in rows are dense consonants
stuck on endless lawns to strangle the verbs
of space and open vista, deny the sound its ricochet.
The walled gardens for lilac and tousled herbs
are jarred by rampant rag-worth, tree-roots, impudence.

Burnt by the grocer's sons in corduroys
Burnt by the die-hards who never died.
Burnt by the ditch-digger's boys.
Burnt by stable-boys.
Burnt by plough-boys.
Burnt by altar boys.
Burnt by boys.

Holiday Landlady, Greece

I think I'm sleeping in her bed.
On the dressing table framed pictures
of children whose children
could be dead,
a Greek bridegroom, solemn
with grinning brothers,
a careful-looking bride.
The frayed wardrobe
hints of mothballs, hung dresses
like flowery ghosts,
bony corsets.
The squeaky bottom drawer
holds men's woollen cardigans,
stained army uniforms, layered
like suffering.

Yesterday, sun-blasted
and parched in the hot afternoon,
wearing my floor-sucking
flip-flops, my towel rolled up,
I found her alone, muttering to herself,
stretched on a bench,
in the shuttered kitchen,
dressed in her widowed black,
asleep.

Amazed
at how the light was kept
at bay, I felt myself go still
and almost tiptoe,
searching for water,
unsure where the fragments,
the clues to loss might lie
in that day-time dark.

Kilmichael for Tourists

('Savages', The Times, London, 1920)

After firing had continued for some time
and many men were wounded,
overwhelming forces of the ambushers
came out and forcibly disarmed the survivors.
There followed a brutal massacre,
the dead and wounded were hacked
about the head with axes, shot guns
fired into their bodies…savagely mutilated.

Crossley tenders gargled up the road,
diesel fuming at a funeral-pace,
sycamore branches strapped for camouflage.
Eighteen men in military greatcoats, vapoury-breath,
curses and cigarettes, close against the cold,
rifles pointing cloud-ward, helmets off,
auxiliaries dozing with the engines.
They were legless in Macroom the previous night,
raising hell, the stripped homes of suspects.
So far the story has been told before.

The fields were ploughed-open and left.
Loose-stone walls were built higher for cover,
guns readied and oiled with purest memory.
Bullets flew faster than any sound,
opened the first head like a smile,
clicked against metal, flattened tyres.
Gun-thunder followed as reinforcement,
blood darkened greatcoats and trousers,
bodies lay tense as crosses, open-mouthed.

The Times said: *Native, unredeemable, blood-cruel*
instinct, and who could expect any better?
Remember tomahawks, knives, the lifting of scalps.
Not worthy to be counted among the civilized.
Not worthy of us. Not worthy.

Mushatt
(Pharmacist Dublin, 1924)

I make them up cures for corns, bad chests,
the scabies, rat bites, black eyes, head lice.
The lotion kills the lice and anything else living.
Then you fine-comb, catch the freshly killed
between your thumb and fore-finger nails.
A squeeze of blood is a dead-sure sign.

We have a bottle too for the hard catarrh.
Dockers suffer it from the sharp coal dust.
You know the way their lined foreheads frown
from thwarted breath. The stuff could lift
paint from the hull of a coal boat,
make the packed snot come down in ropes.

Two old brothers from the Coombe,
Anto and Gitser, live together, never married,
come in most months to have their nails cut,
fingers and toes. They never speak to each other.
We have sharp scissors and on a quiet day
you'll hear the spat spat of nail bits
hit the far wall. They are hard as bone.
Soft nails don't fly like that.

For a hangover we make up Black Draft,
a mix of senna pods and special salts.
The men queue outside, often in the rain,
on Sunday mornings, no money left to pay.
In the heat of the haggle one says to me:

'Your kind crucified Our Lord and now
you're crucifying me. I wouldn't trust you
further than I could fart into a loud gale.
You'll get no blood money from me.'

By the heel of the next week they pay
the few pennies owed, knowing well
their time of need will come round again.

Walking home on weeknights I meet gangs
on dry, threatening streets, dense packed,
feral, throwing shapes. Francis St, Dean St,
near Fallons at New Row, up Engine Alley,
I am spotted, then known, their stares
can track the pace of my breath, the single river
of their molten lives parts before me like the Jordan.

Shots

One of you in Griffith barracks 1941,
with wiry comrades from Francis St flats,
your underfed pigeon chests
puffed out by ammo pouches,
carbolic scrubbed, girl-shy,
shaving almost weekly.
Enormous rifles like artillery posed
in battle readiness at your feet.
Frayed green uniforms and harp badges
give the game away.

'We were waiting to be posted to Libya,
to be trained by the Desert Rats.
Had to parachute behind the German lines
from twenty thousand feet. Shit inside foxholes
in the dunes, cook fresh vulture in a helmet pot,
pass sand-grains in our sweat,
scrape human tissue from the tracks of tanks.
Our artillery was so fierce whole battalions
of Afrika Corps were cowed in procession,
trucks alight, scalded hands behind their heads.
We didn't even have to point our weapons.'

'How many did ye capture at a time, Da?'

'Hundreds and thousands, nowhere
to feckin' put them.'

2

The ammo pouches look hollow.
The one over-long Enfield
does eight men, the few helmets
are surplus from the Crimea.
Loud grins in ranks for the camera,
soldiers relaxed, unbuttoned, paused
near dry-stone walls and fuchsia.
You're on manoeuvres in furthest Cork.
Field-Marshal Monty's secret reserve,
shouldering cocked and loaded hurleys
on the long march in double ranks,
to the east of Ballincollig.

'Was this one taken after you were in the desert, Da?'

'Sure son, came back to keep an eye on things here.'

Tuscany

Below us the barn door is stuck ajar
since the day its hinges slipped
with the frame's slow rot.

Lizards dart up like shrunken dragons
from the barn's flat straw ground,
take the cleaner air and size us up.

Wood pigeons strut the roof, make
clacking sounds like close gunfire.
Their hollow cooings hint of subtle perils.

Rain-drops panic on the tiles, then stop.
The aftermath sharpens tension.

Outside, swallows fan out, air-warriors
slicing the wind in pairs, then disappear
between clay bricks under eaves.

At dusk we are perched between
bickering birds above, lizardly rustlings below,
the wary in a sandwich of the wild.

Feral dogs bark earthy frustrations out
in the dark. The beasts are waiting
for us, barely beyond our lamps.

Daylight through the shutters announces balance.
You search the Internet on a mobile
for the day's forecast, perhaps an earlier flight.

Soles

I had one pair of shoes when I was seven.
When I had to make my Holy Communion,
my father cut up a Woodbine box
and stuck the cardboard inside the shoes
to cover two big holes.

I got the wafer, dry as paper in my mouth
and when the priest said to kneel for the Confiteor,
I stayed standing, pressing on the cardboard.

The other girls rose and knelt
and rose around me like a white sea
showing off their new soles.

Music

Through our dazed windows the other cars
were floating on the shoreline sand,
the sea a sullen stranger not far off.
We peeled each other back to a raw gift,
not flesh, not skin, but a new, not wholly expected
innocence, a fresh unreadable music.

Our nakedness was cluttered by coats and bags,
discarded balled-up jeans, stripy cheesecloth,
stubborn gear-stick, humpy console, the remnants
of sandwich-in-paper-bag lunches, empty Evian.
It was French-kissing in a musty wardrobe.
It was drinking red wine from a cracked tooth-mug.

The night conspired with us, the lit dashboard
was a map with numbers, the couples either side
strung along the strand, boggling car-springs,
performed an unanimous mime orchestra:
cellos marking time, edgy violins, insistent drums,
that sudden flurry on strings, a self-satisfied oboe.

Pause

Stay tuned to the slow ricochet of leaves,
the way forest wind plays with your clothes,
the kind of breathing that synchs with your pulse,
and you'll begin to know the careful deep sigh,
the tiny strangle in your hollows, the pull and tug
of flesh's insults, its stored defeats, the drag and drop
of partings, the being left out, straight losses
the ultimate forgetting still to come.

Stay longer until that breath-pulse tires your sense
and tires more 'til all that's left is quiet,
a thin breathless quiet outside flesh's history,
and let it sit, and you sit still inside it, don't waste
the moment, this gift, this unfleshed nothing, now.

Knowing
(Inspired by a Mr Rumsfeld)

As we know, there are known knowns.
There are things we know that we know.
Like the fall of night, the light from candles,
the way afterwards you turn on your side,
smoothed out, still within range, gathered.

We also know that there are known unknowns,
that is to say there are some things we know
we don't know. Where you hide in my presence,
your location in the dark, how sleep eludes us,
why loss enlarges unbidden. Gathers.

There are also unknown unknowns,
the facts we don't know we don't know.
Whisper them, ring true.

Chaos for Beginners

The boys wore the look of pending combat.
They heaped tyres and sticks, factory-pallets,
tree branches, someone's mislaid fence.
The tyres stacked high burned best
and brightest. Satisfying black smoke
fell over roofs and empty streets.

All the rudiments of battle: harmonies
massacred, no survivors on the enemy side,
a sense of heat and purpose, sounds
beyond senses or control, swollen cries,
threats against the elements, the wind,
against darkness and the cynical gods.

The bonfire stayed lit all night,
a glow-worry marking the edge
of fresh-mopped suburb, of windows
in rows locked smoke-tight; the edge too
of unbuilt scrub, feral wasteland.

The boys stood around in t-shirts
or hunkered down with fag butts,
facing the flames, practicing menace,
firelight pooling youth at their throats.

Making-Up

Her powder compact was on the mantelpiece,
eye pencils, clips, slides, mysterious tubes
by L'Oréal, a pink bag with jumbled hairnets
my side of the coal scuttle.
She used the gilt mirror, eye-high
over the kitchen fireplace,
and not her private sit-down
bedroom dressing-table.

Before the weekly outing with her sister
were moments of deepening and defining.
Cheeks became a more intense
reddy-cream, eyebrows made to stand out
against the lighter lashes, lips unreasonably
crimson, ears festooned with dangly pearls.
Hair, imprisoned in rollers and clips
for half a day, was let loose over her shoulders
in a shake of curls on borrowed curl-time.
Odd grey hairs, strayed from the dye,
were tweezered, then individually cut.

Now we have come
to the end of seeing
and of making afresh.
I'm the eye-high mirror
screwed tight to the wall,
holding her image,
gilt-edged, spotted,
stubborn.

Museum

1 Fillings

In the Washington Holocaust Museum
there's a stone table, etched and stained,
used for extracting gold fillings
from the grey mouths of the gassed.
There's a circular hole cut in the stone
at the top, like in a massage table,
where the head was laid
to keep it comfortable and steady.

If the gold was buried in the stubborn
molars at the back, they snipped off
the lower jaw using short-stemmed
bolt cutters, designed for barbed wire.

2 Shoes

On another floor brown hillocks
of shoes, sandals, boots
preserve the sweat and fungus of the dead.
The sandals' laces are untied,
taken off carefully by bathers
so as not to mark the bathroom floor.
I spot a pair of stilettos in a twisted
jumble of leather.

3 Stars

In the photograph a resigned old man,
black hair matted to his skull
by rain or sweat, kneels at the pit.
As proof you can erase by branding,
there's a Star of David on his coat,
the muzzle of a pistol at his ear.
The uniformed pistol-holder looks bored
in that deadly adolescent way.